THE MAGIC OF CHILDREN

THE MAGIC

BEAUTIFUL WRITINGS
ABOUT
THE WONDERFUL WORLD
OF CHILDREN

OF CHILDREN

WITH PHOTOGRAPHS
BY PHOEBE DUNN

EDITED BY KITTY CLEVENGER
AND AILEENE NEIGHBORS

♛ HALLMARK CROWN EDITIONS

ACKNOWLEDGMENTS

"Worth the Price" from "A Child's Garden of Manners" in *The Snake Has All the Lines* by Jean Kerr. Copyright © 1959 by The Curtis Publishing Company. Reprinted by permission of Doubleday Publishing Company. "Child's Country" by Kenneth L. Patton from *The Visitor and Hello Man,* Copyright © 1947. Reprinted by permission Kenneth L. Patton. "The Joy of Children" from *The Joy of Children* by Pearl S. Buck. Copyright © 1964 by Pearl S. Buck. Reprinted by permission of Harold Ober Associates Incorporated. "A Child's Wonder" from pp. 42-44 *The Sense of Wonder* by Rachel Carson. Copyright 1956 by Rachel Carson. By permission of Harper & Row, Publishers, Inc. "The Fishing Pole" from "A Little Freckled Person" by Mary Carolyn Davies. Copyright 1947 by Mary Carolyn Davies. Reprinted by permission of Houghton Mifflin Company. "First Day of School" from *I Wonder How, I Wonder Why* by Aileen Fisher. Copyright 1962 by Aileen Fisher. Reprinted by permission of Abelard-Schuman Limited. "What Is a Child?" by Paul Engle. Reprinted by permission of the author. Quote by Walter Schirra, Sr. Reprinted by permission of the author. "Lemonade Stand" first published in *Story Parade,* 1954; copyright reassigned to Dorothy Brown Thompson. Used by permission of Dorothy Brown Thompson. Matthew 18:1-4 from the *Revised Standard Version Bible.* Reprinted by permission of The National Council of the Churches of Christ. Excerpt by Jacqueline Kennedy Onassis from *Common Sense Wisdom of Three First Ladies* by Bill Adler. Reprinted by permission of Bill Adler. "Me" from *The Complete Poems of Walter de la Mare, 1970.* Reprinted by permission of The Viking Press, Inc.; The Literary Trustees of Walter de la Mare; and The Society of Authors as their representative. "Our Visible Immortality" from *Baby and Child Care* by Benjamin Spock, M.D. © 1945, 1946, 1957 by Benjamin Spock. Reprinted by permission of Simon & Schuster, Inc., Pocket Books Division.

THE MAGIC OF CHILDREN

THIS IS A CHILD

Kay Andrew

A child is innocence meeting the world
With a trusting, out-stretched hand,
Curiosity discovering the world
Unhurriedly, unplanned,
Honesty laying bare the world's
True joys and hidden flaws,
Excitement never allowing the world
To stop, but briefly pause.
A child is Laughter conquering the world
With an open, smiling face.
A child is Love uplifting the world
To a happier, higher place.

OUR VISIBLE IMMORTALITY

Benjamin Spock

Parents have children because...they love children and want some of their very own. They also love children because they remember being loved so much by their parents in their own childhood. Taking care of their children, seeing them grow and develop into fine people, gives most parents—despite the hard work—their greatest satisfaction in life. This is creation. This is our visible immortality. Pride in other worldly accomplishments is usually weak in comparison.

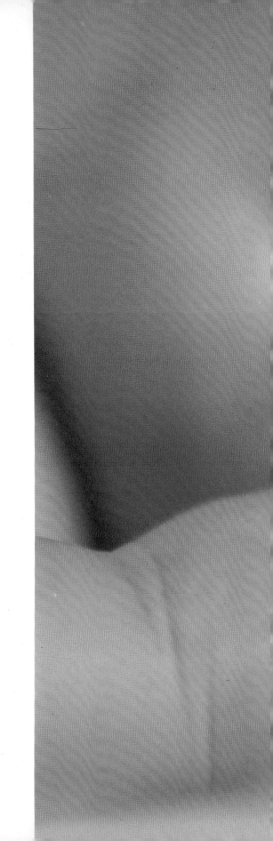

George Gordon, Lord Byron

He smiles and sleeps!—sleep on
And smile, thou little, young inheritor
Of a world scarce less young: sleep on and smile!
Thine are the hours and days when both are cheering
And innocent!

DANDELIONS

Mary A. Loberg

What child hasn't picked them once
or taken home bouquets,
whistled through their hollow stems
on lazy, sunny days,
braided sticky necklaces
or made a friendship ring?

What child hasn't blown the puff
to watch the seeds take wing
...from these golden buttons
sewn upon the coat of Spring?

WORTH THE PRICE

Jean Kerr

Children have such a lively sense of the inviolability of what belongs to them (as you've noticed if you ever tried to throw out an old coloring book) that it should be easy for them to remember that adults, too, have little fetishes about their personal possessions ("You don't like anybody to play with your tractor, do you? Well, Daddy doesn't like anybody to play with his tape recorder.").

Sometimes it's hard to know just what to say. Last winter I found on the breakfast table a letter addressed to Mommy Kerr. It was on my very best stationery, and there were ten brand-new four-cent stamps plastered all over the envelope. When I pulled out the letter, the message read:

Dear Mommy,

John is mad at you becuase you won't let us put our snowballs in the freeser but I am not mad at you becuase I love you

Your Frend, Colin

Well, there you are. When you get right down to it, it was worth forty cents.

Walter Schirra, Sr.

You don't raise heroes, you raise sons.
And if you treat them like sons, they'll
turn out to be heroes, even if it's just in
your own eyes.

LITTLE GIRL'S WORLD

Reginald Holmes

Blue jeans and sneakers, hair tightly curled,
One little girl and a make-believe world,
Adores playing house or shopping downtown,
Make-believe weddings, a lace curtain gown.

She's trying to learn to cook and to sew,
All the things a young lady should know;
But more efficient, as folks will agree
At skipping a rope or climbing a tree.

She faces each day with a smile on her face
And leaves happy memories time can't erase.
The future is shaped with the feminine art
From dreams that lie in a little girl's heart.

John Milton

Childhood shows the man as morning does the day.

CHILD AT THE SEASHORE

Kay Wissinger

I watched the child upon the strand,
Her face with ecstasy alight,
Holding within her small cupped hand
A treasure for her heart's delight.

The lapping waves, the sea gulls' play,
Far out, the ocean's rise and swell,
The golden wonder of the day,
She captured in one fragile shell.

Barbara Kunz Loots

A little boy's world is a place to have fun in—
To climb on, dig into, jump over, and run in—
As venturesome as the games he plays,
And as timeless as each of his carefree days.

It's filled with the everyday things he likes:
Puppies, ice cream, baseballs and bikes;
Things that roll or crawl or fly;
Paths to explore, "double dares" to try.

It's a place to learn what he needs to know,
To laugh, to think, to watch and grow;
For a little boy's world, as small as it seems,
Is as broad as the future, as high as his dreams!

Persian Proverb

Children are a bridge to heaven.

THE JOY OF CHILDREN

Pearl Buck

It is a joy which holds the world together, the joy of children. Children are world treasures. However far I travel, into the uttermost parts of the earth, I find the same love of children that enriches our own life here in the United States. Indian mothers and fathers in a remote village in Rajasthan love their children in the same way that American parents love their own. It is a love necessary to the fulfillment of life. The individual human cycle is not whole until man and woman look back to the parents who gave them life and forward to the children to whom they themselves give life. Only thus does the individual feel assured of his place in the eternal scheme of creation. Only thus does his heart find rest.

ME

Walter de la Mare

As long as I live
I shall always be
My Self — and no other,
Just me.

Like a tree.

Like a willow or elder,
An aspen, a thorn,
Or a cypress forlorn.

Like a flower,
For its hour
A primrose, a pink,
Or a violet —
Sunned by the sun,
And with dewdrops wet.
Always just me.

KNOW YOU
WHAT IT IS TO BE A CHILD?

Francis Thompson

Know you what it is to be a child?...It is to be so little that the elves can reach to whisper in your ear. It is to turn pumpkins into coaches, and mice into horses, lowness into loftiness and nothing into everything—for each child has his fairy godmother in his own soul. It is to live in a nutshell and count yourself king of the infinite space; it is

To see a world in a grain of sand,
Heaven in a wild flower,
To hold infinity in the palm of
your hand,
And Eternity in an hour.

Mary Carolyn Davies

A fishing pole's a curious thing;
It's made of just a stick and string;
A boy at one end and a wish,
And on the other end a fish.

THE GREATEST OF ALL

Matthew 18:1-4 (RSVB)

At that time the disciples came to Jesus, saying, "Who is the greatest in the kingdom of heaven?" And calling to him a child, he put him in the midst of them, and said, "Truly, I say to you, unless you turn and become like children, you will never enter the kingdom of heaven. Whoever humbles himself like this child, he is the greatest in the kingdom of heaven."

Remy de Gourmont

The little girl expects no declaration
of tenderness from her doll.
She loves it, and that's all.
It is thus that we should love.

LEMONADE STAND

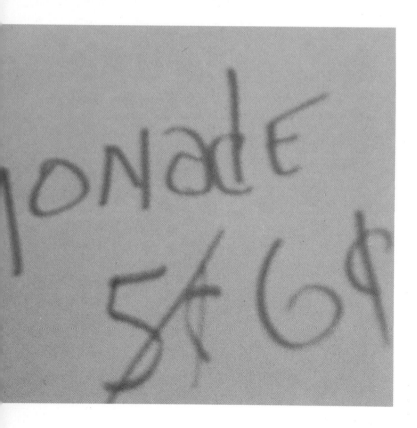

Dorothy Brown Thompson

Come and buy —
Have a try!
Throats are thirsty in July!

You who pass
Sip a glass,
Cold as snow and fresh as grass!

Sharp and sweet,
It's a treat,
You'll forget the summer heat!

Going far?
Stop your car.
Just a nickel — here you are!

WISDOM

Hildegarde Hawthorne

Sometimes, looking deep into the eyes of a child, you are conscious of meeting a glance full of wisdom. The child has known nothing yet but love and beauty.... And yet you meet this wonderful look that tells you in a moment more than all the years of experience have seemed to teach.

CHILD'S COUNTRY

Kenneth L. Patton

Nothing is strange to the child for whom everything is new.
Where all things are new nothing is novel.
The child does not yet know what belongs and what does not;
   therefore for him all things belong.
The ear of the child is open to all music.
His eyes are open to all arts.
His mind is open to all tongues.
His being is open to all manners.
In the child's country there are no foreigners.

PUDDLES

Louise Hajek

Puddles are little lakes to wade in,
Not deep enough to be afraid in.
Puddles are made quick as a flash
By raindrops bouncing splishity splash.
Puddles are playmates, puddles are fun
But they run away when they see the sun.

CHILDHOOD DREAMS

Charles Dickens

The dreams of childhood—its airy fables, its graceful, beautiful, humane, impossible adornments of the world beyond: so good to be believed in once, so good to be remembered when outgrown.

MY SHADOW

Robert Louis Stevenson

I have a little shadow that goes in and out with me,
And what can be the use of him is more than I can see.
He is very, very like me from the heels up to the head;
And I see him jump before me, when I jump into my bed.

The funniest thing about him is the way he likes to grow—
Not at all like proper children, which is always very slow;
For he sometimes shoots up taller like an india-rubber ball,
And he sometimes gets so little that there's none of him at all.

Margaret Mead

Grandparents need grandchildren to keep the changing world alive for them. And grandchildren need grandparents to help them know who they are and to give them a sense of human experience in a world they cannot know. In the past this was literally so. Now and in the future, when more adults will be concerned with the care of young children who are not their own descendants, this remains a model of mutual learning across generations.

FIRST DAY OF SCHOOL

Aileen Fisher

I wonder
if my drawing
will be as good as theirs.

I wonder
if they'll like me
or just be full of stares.

I wonder
if my teacher
will look like Mom or Gram.

I wonder
if my puppy
will wonder
where I am.

CURIOSITY

Harry Behn

Tell me, tell me everything!
What makes it Winter
And then Spring?
Which are the children
Butterflies?
Why do people keep
Winking their eyes?
Where do birds sleep?
Do bees like to sting?
Tell me, tell me please, everything!

Tell me, tell me, I want to know!
What makes leaves grow
In the shapes they grow?
Why do goldfish
Keep chewing? and rabbits
Warble their noses?
Just from habits?
Where does the wind
When it goes away go?
Tell me, or don't even grown-ups know?

Jacqueline Kennedy Onassis

Once you have a child,
you don't think of yourself so much
but of the generation ahead.
Any sacrifice is made with joy.

Jacqueline Kennedy Onassis

TO BE A CHILD

Paul Engle

This is to be a child: To heighten
Each thing you handle, to be shyer
Than rabbit in wide field, to frighten
Deep dark that scared you, to fly higher
Than kite or hunting hawk, to brighten
Daylight, because you are a fire.

A CHILD'S WONDER

Rachel Carson

A child's world is fresh and new and beautiful, full of wonder and excitement. It is our misfortune that for most of us that clear-eyed vision, that true instinct for what is beautiful and awe-inspiring, is dimmed and even lost before we reach adulthood.

If I had influence with the good fairy who is supposed to preside over the christening of all children, I should ask that her gift to each child in the world be a sense of wonder so indestructible that it would last throughout life, as an unfailing antidote against the boredom and disenchantment of later years, the sterile preoccupation with things that are artificial, the alienation from the sources of our strength.

If a child is to keep alive his inborn sense of wonder without any such gift from the fairies, he needs the companionship of at least one adult who can share it, rediscovering with him the joy, excitement and mystery of the world we live in.

Text set in linofilm Optima by Western Typesetting Service.
Titles set in handset Weiss II by Rochester Typographic Company.
Designed by Ronald E. Garman.